ALLEYS IN BEIJING

北京胡同

FOREIGN LANGUAGES PRESS   BEIJING

外文出版社 北京

ALLEYS IN BEIJING

Born and bred in Beijing and having spent more than a half century of my life here, I probably qualify to be a "real old Beijinger".

What is most unforgettable in Beijing? It is the many long and short, wide and narrow alleys and lanes. Whenever I go on a trip away from home, particularly on a trip abroad, what I miss most are the ancient, elegant, familiar, lovable and plain lanes. In other words, unless I am back in the lanes, I have not returned home. Home is inseparable from the alleys and lanes. Nor is Beijing separable from them. To a certain extent, the alleys and lanes are the soul of Beijing.

Then just how many alleys and lanes are there in Beijing? Veteran residents say: "The major ones number 360 and small ones are as many as hairs on an ox." Men of letters have used the term of several thousand to describe the lanes. According to incomplete statistics, by 1949, there had been a total of over 6,000 lanes within the boundary of Beijing, out of which over 4,550 were located in the inner city districts. Naturally, the figure for today is much more impressive than that.

In my view, the term "culture" probably refers to a particular way of life. People of different times have different ways of life and thus live in different cultures. In this sense, for generations, people in Beijing have lived in a culture of lanes. As time goes by, especially with the progress of urban construction, lanes in Beijing are decreasing in number. On their ground, tall buildings are springing up. It is against this background, Shen Yantai and Wang Changqing, the couple photographers, have presented readers with this collection of *Alleys in Beijing*. Just as they state it in the "Afterword" of this work, they were not prepared "for the sudden disappearing of the lanes which have presented a culture of a particular historic time. We feel it an urgent task to capture the sights and sounds through the camera lens, recording the historic footprints of the culture of lanes in this ancient capital city, the myriad vistas of people, their typical ways of life and customs and habits unique to these lanes. Our contribution may not amount to much of a creative surprise. It was meant an attempt to rescue a cultural heritage, collecting data of images for people to do research and studies of a passing culture in the future. We found this a worthwhile job, though it was hard and cost a lot of time and sweat. In doing so, we were not going after monetary payment, or an award of any kind, but simply driven by a sense of duty. " Reading these words, shouldn't we cheer them for their rescue operation?

Having read the book, I was profoundly moved by "fiery" passions that are present throughout the work.

First, the passion of the photographers.

Interestingly, neither of the couple is a native of Beijing, as he was born in Shanghai in the south and she in Taiyuan, Shanxi, west of Beijing. But they all have lived for many years in Beijing and more importantly cherish a deep love of the city. They have a particular sentiment for the alleys and lanes here and their hearts beat to the rhythm of life in the alleys and lanes. To a certain extent, the lanes have become part of their life. As a result, when they focus their camera on the lanes, their own passion goes into their work, thus arousing a strong response from whoever sees their work. When I looked at their photos, I could not help thinking that what I was actually seeing was the abstract but ubiquitous souls of the photographers rather than the concrete images in the photographs. I believe this passion and sentiment are the most valuable and irreplaceable qualities of an artist, which renders the works with a strong vitality.

Second, the passion and sentiment in the works.

It can be said that every picture in the book, with or without people in it, whether taken in the spring sunshine, summer rain, autumn wind or winter snow, focuses on the people and thus on the sentiment in the alleyways. I want to particularly point out that the photographers have displayed a boundless love and longing for the alleys and lanes in Beijing through their pictures. They told this encounter. One day they walked in an old quadrangle house which was being torn down and saw an elderly man standing in front of broken walls. His entirely family had moved into a new apartment building, but he was reluctant to part with the soon-to-disappear dwellings, where perhaps he had spent his life of childhood, youth, middleage and part of his senior years. He looked as if he wanted to cry, but managed to hold back his tears. He wanted to say something but words failed him. His last act was to pick and take away with him the last ripen Chinese wolfberry fruit. Perhaps it was this discovery with a shattering impact that gave them the inspiration for the picture entitled "Difficult to part with the old house". In this photo, an old man stood in front of a broken wall in a deadly quiet surrounding. He stared at what was in front of him with a helpless expression on the face. His mouth seemed to be moving but no words came out.... Works like this lead readers to vividly feel that the old man seems to just have had a heart-to-heart and moving conversation with the photographers. I remember the great writer Tolstoy once said that the impact of art was determined by three elements in the work and two of them being "the unique characteristics of the sentiment it conveys" and "the explicitness of such sentiment it conveys". The artistic impact of this photo is so enormous and profound that readers will find it hard to forget.

Finally, let me congratulate the publication of *Alleys in Beijing*. I look forward to seeing more, newer and better works from the two author-photographers.

In photography, I am a layman. What I have written is therefore an observation of an ordinary reader.

I thank the authors and the readers.

北 京 胡 同

　　笔者生在北京，长在北京，半个多世纪过去了，大约算得上是个地道的"老北京"。北京城里最使人难以忘怀的是什么呢？就是那大大小小的、在南方被叫做街巷的胡同。每当我从外地特别是从外国出差归来的时候，最急于想见到的便是那一条条古朴的、幽雅的、熟悉的、亲切的胡同。或者说，只有见到了这些胡同才能算是回到了北京，回到了家。胡同与家分不开，北京与胡同分不开。一定意义上说，胡同就是北京的魂。

　　据说，"胡同"一词出现在金、元时代，来源于蒙古语系，是女真人和蒙古人进入中原以后，按照自己的习惯把城市的街巷称为"胡同"的。那么，北京到底有多少胡同呢？听老人们说："大胡同三百六，小胡同如牛毛。"意思是，多得数也数不清。为此，文人们也有"庶五城胡同，浩繁几千条之间"一说。根据不完全的统计，北京全城到1949年为止，已经有胡同6000多条，城区里的胡同有4550多条。自然，现在又要比这个数字大得多了。到底有多少，似乎谁也说不清。

　　我以为，所谓"文化"，大约就是人们的一种生活方式，不同的时代人们有着不同的生活方式，也就有着不同的文化。或许从这个角度来看，北京人正是祖祖辈辈生活在"胡同文化"里的。随着时代的发展，特别是随着城市建设的发展，北京城的胡同越来越少，代之为一栋栋高楼大厦。正是在这种情况下，沈延太、王长青两位摄影家把这本《北京胡同》画册奉献给广大读者。正如他们所言："我们深为胡同作为一个特定历史时代的文化的不辞而别而感到措手不及，胡同文化的面貌急待用摄影纪实的手法'留真'下来。尽我们微薄的力量留下一些古都胡同文化的历史陈迹，胡同天地里的百姓世相，京味京韵的民俗风情和市井氛围，虽算不上惊人的创作，却干了一点抢救遗产的活儿，为后来者追寻、研究即将逝去的胡同文化，留一点形象的资料。这是摄影力所能及的一种功能，作为从事摄影的苦力，流点汗也是值得的，不求报酬，不图奖赏，责任感的驱使，仅此而已。"读到这里，难道我们还不应该为他们的"抢救"，为他们的"留真"拍手叫好，倍加称赞吗？

　　我看过画册以后，深深地被一个像火一样燃烧着的"情"字所吸引，所打动，所感染。

首先说作者的情。

说来也巧，两位摄影家都不是土著的北京人，一位生于江南的上海，一位生于山西的太原。然而，他们都久居北京，更重要的是热爱北京，他们对北京城的胡同情有独钟，息息相关，一定意义上说，胡同已经成了他们生命的一部分。因此，他们在用手中照相机进行纪实留真的时候，就不能不融进了自己沉甸甸的情感，从而使读者也得到强烈的共鸣。在欣赏作品的时候我就想，与其说是看到了照片上的具体形象，不如说是看到了作者那抽象的又无所不在的灵魂。我以为，这些也许是一个艺术创作者最可宝贵的东西，不可代替的东西，使作品能够富有强大生命力的东西。

其次说作品的情。

可以说，这里的每一幅作品，不管是有人物出现的，没人物出现的，也不管是在春光里、夏雨里，秋风里，冬雪里，作者始终把镜头对准了胡同里的人。因而，也就把镜头对准了情。我想特别要指出的是，作者通过作品表现出一种对于京城胡同的无限眷恋之情。作者讲了这样一件事——有一天，他们走进了一片正在拆迁的四合院老房子之间，看见在已经拆毁的断墙残壁前站着一位老人，他的全家已经搬进新建的公寓楼房，可他还是恋恋不舍地来看看这些行将消失的老房子，也许他就是在这座老房子里生，老房子里长的，老房子里留下了他的童年，他的青年，他的中年，和他的一部分老年，他欲言又止，欲哭无泪，最后摘走了老院子里最后一束红透的枸杞子。大约正是这个具有震撼力的形象发现，使得他们创作了《故宅难舍》那幅照片。那里也有一位老人，也是站在已经拆毁的断墙残壁跟前，周围安静得没有一点声音，他双目凝视着眼前的一切，脸上呈现出有些茫然的表情，蠕动的嘴里仿佛有着说不出又说不尽的话……这些使读者真切地感觉到，老人似乎是刚刚和作者进行过一次推心置腹的，又激动万分的谈话。记得，大作家托尔斯泰说过，艺术感染力大小、深浅，取决于作品表现出的三个要素，其中的两个便是"所传达的感情具有多么大的独特性"和"这种感情的传达有多么清晰"。应当说，这幅照片的艺术感染力是大的，是深的，是使读者容易记住又不忍心忘掉的。

最后，我要衷心地祝贺《北京胡同》的出版，并企盼将来能够看到两位作者更新、更好、更多的作品问世。对于摄影艺术我是个外行，说不出什么精彩的意见来，写在这里的只不过是一个普通读者的观后感而已。

谢谢作者，也谢谢读者。

A bird's eye view of the intricate structures in the Forbidden City which were arranged in one after another courtyards of quadrangle houses. The paths and passages along the palace walls resemble alleys and lanes in civilian living quarters. The real differences lie in the terrible quietness and a cold solemnity and the absence of freedom and friendship.

俯瞰紫禁城可以看出，里面的重重宫阙犹如一座座四合院，宫墙夹峙下的宫街、宫巷，形同民间的胡同，只是徒有森严与冷寂，缺少温馨与自如。

Connoisseurs grace the antique stand at the morning market.

早市上的古董摊常有行家光顾。

8

A morning market next to the palace wall. The appearance of markets like this in recent years in Beijing makes shopping easier for the residents.

临护城河而设的早市，每天拂晓开市，近午即散。

The lanes next to the Forbidden City appeared after the royal palace opened to the public, thus they were, relatively speaking, younger members of the family of alleys and lanes.

紧傍紫禁城的胡同。它们应形成于紫禁城开禁以后，是胡同家族中的新生代。

Just imagine the fun of a tour along the moat on such a tricycle.

乘坐这种人力三轮车沿护城河游览，别有情趣。

"Check, mate!" A match at the foot of the Forbiden City.

紫禁城下布阵对弈。

The trees by the palace wall are a sanctuary for both men and birds.

人和鸟都喜欢这傍着宫墙的林荫深处。

A view out of the window of a residential house at Beichizi. Across the moat on the east and west sides of the Forbidden City, are Nanchizi (South Pool) and Beichizi (North Pool) and Nanchang (South Long) Street and Beichang (North Long) Street. People living in these places do not have to go out of their house to take a look at the Forbidden City.

北池子一居民家的窗外景色。紫禁城东西两侧护城河的对岸，分别是南、北池子和南、北长街，住在这里的居民足不出户就能观赏到宫城里的景物。

The bushes and trees along the moat and the refreshing air they generate draw residents from the nearby alleys and lanes to come and do physical exercises. It is also a favorite spot for lovers.

护城河畔林木葱郁，清幽宜人。附近胡同里的居民早晚喜欢来此练拳健身，散步消闲；情侣们也视此为约会的绝佳之处。

The lane east of the Lamaist White Pagoda in Miaoying Temple which is also known as the White Pagoda Temple. The lane on which the temple sits is called White Pagoda Lane.

白塔寺东夹道。妙应寺内有一座喇嘛式白塔，所以寺又名白塔寺，它所在的胡同则名白塔巷。白塔寺东夹道位于白塔巷以东。

Lanes and houses near Miaoying Temple east of Fuchengmen in the West District. The temple, with a towering white pagoda built in 1279, stands in sharp contrast with the surrounding houses.

西城阜成门内妙应寺下的胡同。妙应寺建成公元 1279 年，其周围的胡同格局与之同时形成。

To admit light and facilitate communication at the time, city planners of the Yuan Dynasty set the width of the lanes in Beijing to be something equalling 9.24 meters. Even in winter, the lanes were filled up with sunlight so long as the weather was fine.

为了宜于通行和采光，元代规划的城区胡同宽度约为9.24米，由于两旁房舍低矮，即使在冬季，只要是晴和的日子，胡同里便充满阳光。

On both sides of this lane are quadrangle houses with entrances opening to the lane. Windows on the back wall of the house tend to be small, indicating the inward-looking and closed-off architectural style of these houses.

胡同两旁是古城传统的民居——四合院。院门临胡同；窗户开在墙壁上方，而且较小，呈现出内向、封闭的特点。

The gate tower at Qianmen, long regarded as the symbol of old Beijing. With its official name as Zhengyangmen, the gate to the center-south of Tiananmen was once the main entrance into Beijing proper. Since the 15th century, the street outside the gate has been a major commercial center in the capital.

被视为旧京象征的前门城楼。前门正名为正阳门，是北京内城的正门，位于天安门正南面。前门外大街早在十五世纪时就成为京城重要的商业区。

Called Zhubaoshi or Jewelry Market, this lane was evolved from a trading ground specializing in jewelry. There are nearly one hundred lanes radiating from the east and west sides of the Outer Qianmen Street, serving as one of the most compact and busiest commercial centers in Beijing. Many of the lanes grew from markets and fairs. Apart from the Jewelry Market, there are such lanes as Liangshidian (Grain Store), Meishi (Coal Market), Zhushikou (Jewelry Market Entrance), Roushi Street (Meat Market Street) and Xianyukou (Fresh Fish Market Entrance).

由古代的珠宝市场衍变成的胡同——珠宝市。前门外大街东、西两侧排列着数以百计的胡同，是京城内胡同最密集的地区之一。这里的胡同有许多是由当年的集市演变而成的，除珠宝市外，尚有粮食店、煤市街、珠市口、肉市街、鲜鱼口等。

Stretching 370 meters, Dashilan Lane is home to a great number of traditionally famous stores including the Tongrentang Chinese Pharmaceutical Store, Ruifuxiang Cloth Shop, Neiliansheng Shoe Store and Zhangyiyuan Tea Shop.

大栅栏全长370米，两旁尽商铺，而且多是蜚声中外的老字号，如同仁堂中药店、瑞蚨祥绸布店、内联升鞋店、张一元茶叶店等。

This old shop in Grain Store Street sells a local flavor soup, *dou zhi*. Made from green beans, the soup has a special strong taste that many veteran Beijing residents love.

粮食店街内的豆汁老铺。豆汁是用绿豆制成的浆汁，味道特异，嗜食者多为京城老居民。

Liangshidian (Grain Store) Street which cuts across Dashilan Lane. In the restaurants and shops on this lane, you can find just about every kind of traditional Beijing local delicacies.

与大栅栏相通的粮食店街。街内餐馆、食肆相接，北京的风味小吃应有尽有。

Outside the Qianmen Gate, Qingfeng Lane, a small and quiet alleyway with very little traffic. Consequently, kids can play in the lane, do graffiti on the wall and the elderly can enjoy their peace as well.

青风巷摄趣。青风巷是前门外一条僻静的小胡同，过往行人、车辆稀少，因此，儿童得以在巷中嬉戏，在壁上涂鸦；老人能够安坐无扰。

Niujie Street and an offshoot lane. Inside Guang'anmen Gate in southwestern part of the city is a north-south street called Niujie where Moslems in Beijing live in a compact community.

牛街及通向街内的胡同之一。城区西南部的广安门内，有一条纵向的街道，名为牛街，是京城内的回族聚居区。牛街西侧由北至南排列着众多小胡同，也多以"牛街X条"命名。

Elderly people dressed in Chinese Moslem attire is a common sight on this street.

漫步牛街，不时可见穿民族服装的回族老人走过。

The mosque at Niujie Street is a symbol of the community. Built in 995, it is the largest and oldest of its kind in Beijing.

牛街礼拜寺临街而立，成为牛街具有象征性的景观。寺建于公元995年，其规模与历史，皆为京城清真寺之冠。

Kongshantang and Baocuitang, two old shops dealing in antiques and jade ware.

琉璃厂内专营古玩、玉器的两家老铺——孔膳堂和宝翠堂。

◁ The 750-meter-long cultural street called Liulichang (Glazed Tile Factory) was built actually on the site of kilns producing glazed tiles for the imperial palace, The well-known stores selling traditional paintings, calligraphy works, stationery, ancient books and antiques almost are all found on this street.

古文化街琉璃厂是在为皇家烧制琉璃瓦件的窑址上兴建的，长750米。京城内销售字画、珍宝、文具、书籍等的名店几乎全集中于此。

24

Interior of the theater that has been restored. Once again, people now can watch opera performances here.

修复后的戏楼内景。戏楼重现往日风貌，人们又可在此品茗观戏。

The diagonal Yandai (Smoking Pipe) Street, east of the Silver Ingot Bridge, twists and turns several times. Diagonal lanes like this usually were found along rivers, lakes, ditches and canals.

银锭桥以东的烟袋斜街。这是一条一街三折的斜向胡同。城区内这类斜胡同屈指可数，当初大都是沿着河、湖、沟、渠的堤岸辟建的。

Yinding (Silver Ingot) Bridge crossing the merging point of Front Shishahai Lake and Houhai Lake. During the 13th century, the area near the bridge was already a major commercial district in the Yuan capital. Lanes extended from the bridge and every house faced the lake, presenting a unique sight.

横跨于什刹前海与后海交汇处的银锭桥。银锭桥一带在十三世纪时就已是元大都城内的主要商业区。桥两旁的胡同沿湖岸延展，家家宅门临水，景色宛若江南。

A lane linking the bell and drum towers which are about a hundred meters apart with the Bell Tower in the north of the Drum Tower. In three stories totalling 46.7 meters, the Drum Tower was built in 1400. The second story used to house one large drum and twenty-four smaller ones, all for the purpose of telling the time.

连接钟鼓楼的胡同。鼓楼位于钟楼以南，两楼相距约百米。鼓楼建于公元1400年，高46.7米，共三层。第二层上原有大鼓一面，小鼓24面，均为古时报时而设。

Zhonglouwan (Bell Tower Twist) Lane next to the Bell Tower which stands at the north end of what used to be the central line of the ancient capital. The tower was first erected in 1272 and rebuilt in 1420. This 47.9-meter-high structure houses a big bronze bell of 5.4 meters in height. In the past, the bell was sounded twice daily, in the morning and evening, to tell the time for city dwellers.

钟楼下的钟楼湾胡同。钟楼矗立于京城中轴线的北端，始建于公元1272年，公元1420年重建。楼高47.9米，内置高5.4米的铜钟。古时每日早晚撞钟报时，城中军民、文武官员闻晨钟而起，闻晚钟而息。

A typical scene in lanes at the foot of the bell and drum towers. Though residents of today no longer follow the bell and drum sound in arranging their activities, they lead an orderly life.

钟鼓楼下胡同里的景象

Laku (Wax Warehouse) Lane still protected by animal guardians. Carved into shapes of animal heads and placed at house gates or lane entrances, the stone sculptures used to symbolize guards in keeping with an ancient tradition. Nowadays they are very rare in Beijing.

有石敢当镇守的腊库胡同。石敢当是中国民间的驱邪镇宅之物，用石料雕成兽头形状，安置在宅门上或街巷入口处，如今，在北京已成为稀有之物。

In the morning, the food stands in a lane called West Xinglong Street are packed with customers. A tricycle rider is looking for his customers.

西兴隆街的早晨。胡同旁的早点摊座无虚席，蹬三轮的工人开始出门揽客。

Now called the Street of Ministry of Foreign Affairs, it used to be called Master Shi's Lane due to the fact that Shi Heng, a senior official of the Ming Dynasty, once had his house here. The residence of Mr. Shi, built in 1456, occupied a quarter of the northern side of the entire lane. In the late years of the Qing Dynasty, it was transferred into a guest house after it had changed hands several times. When Dr. Sun Yat-sen, then president of the new Republic of China, came to Beijing in August 1912, he stayed in this place. In 1913, the Ministry of Foreign Affairs moved in, giving the street the name that has lasted till today.

位居东城繁华地段的外交部街。原名石大人胡同，因胡同内有明代权臣石亨的赐第而得名。石亨府第建于公元1456年，占据胡同北侧四分之一地段。清末，这座几易其主的豪宅被改建为迎宾馆。1912年8月，中华民国第一任总统孙中山来京时曾下榻于此。1913年外交部迁入，胡同易名外交部街。

Zhengyi Road in winter. About one kilometer east of the Tiananmen Square, the road is known for its European architecture, since its neighboring community was once the foreign legions.

正义路冬景。正义路在天安门广场以东约1公里处，由于与旧时的使馆区毗邻，两旁建筑与街景具有欧陆风格。

Xiaojingchang Lane.
小经厂胡同

Jiuwan or the Nine-Turning Lane, called so for being the lane with the most turnings.

拐弯最多的胡同——九弯胡同

Xiaolaba or the Tiny Trumpet Lane is one of the narrowest passageways in Beijing.

最窄的胡同之一——小喇叭胡同

Wow! It's only just over a meter wide.

宽仅 1 米余的胡同。

The South Songnian Lane in the northeast part of the Inner City. It was once known as the Emperor's Son-in-Law Wang's Lane. In the vicinity are the East and West Songnian lanes.

内城东北的南颂年胡同，原名王驸马胡同，与其相邻的尚有东、西颂年胡同。

Winter snow gives a face list for the Fourth Dongsi Lane.

东四四条之冬。胡同披上了银装，呈现出另一番景象。

Snow brings joy to both children and adults in this lane.

冬雪给胡同里的大人和孩子带来了乐趣，打雪仗、堆雪人是儿童们最喜爱的游戏。

A bird's eye view of a medium-sized quadrangle house

中型四合院鸟瞰

34

1. House gate   宅门
2. Screen   影壁
3. Room opposite the main room   倒座房
4. Floral-pendant gate   垂花门
5. Circular corridor   游廊
6. Main room   正房
7. Eastern wing room   东厢房
8. Western wing room   西厢房
9. Courtyard   庭院
10. Side courtyard   跨院

A spacious house entrance. Entrances of quadrangle houses consist of two main categories. One category is built into an entry way of one or several bays. The other is a gate joining two ends of the courtyard walls. The one in this photo belongs to the first category. Both sides of such an entrance have a lot of open space. Obviously, such entrances are found in expensive quadrangle houses. Usually a stone staircase outside the entrance was used for helping people to mount horses.

广亮式宅门。四合院的大门依其建筑形式分为屋宇式和墙垣式两类。前一类由一间或若干间房屋构成，后一类直接在院墙接合处设门。广亮式门属前一类，门设于屋的中柱位置，门内外皆有较宽敞的空间，用于较讲究的四合院。门前大多设有上马石。

Gate of a house on Niujie Street. A gate is built into what otherwise looks like the back of a room. The corner of the top frame and the wall often have bricks with decorations known as *ruyi*, or "as-you-wish" patterns. Thus such gates are known as *ruyi* gates.

牛街某宅大门。是另一种屋宇式的门，门设在外檐柱间，因为门楣与墙的交角处，常砌有如意形的装饰，所以称为如意门。

This is another kind of entrance with two stone stools.

蛮子门是屋宇式门的又一形式，门扉位于外檐两柱之间，门框的四角为直角。

This simple kind of gate has no decorations. It is somehow called "Eagle-will-not-alight" gate.

鹰不落式院门。属墙垣式门，无多余的饰件，是较简易的宅门。

This type of entrance, joining two walls and crowned with a gate roof, is often found in small-size quadrangle houses.

墙垣式门之一。门两侧与院墙相接，门上建有门罩。较小型的四合院多采用这类形式的门。

Gates of the house of the relatively well-to-do usually are decorated with door clasps, gate cymbals and protective wrappings. And in front of the entrance, there are also drum stones, stones for tying and mounting horses.

讲究的四合院门扉上饰有门簪、门钹和包叶，门前有上马石、拴马桩和抱鼓石。

Drum stones with varied decorative carvings. The lower part is a stand with a hole for resting the door axle so that the door can turn to open and shut. The drum stone, either in round or square shape, is a decorative object to expel ghost and attract good luck.

纹饰各异的抱鼓石。抱鼓石由位于门内的枕石和门外的抱鼓组成。枕石为方形，上有槽孔，门轴插入孔内，门扇就可以转动开关；抱鼓是门前的饰件，或圆或方，上面雕刻兽形或花卉图案，以驱邪纳吉。

A screen outside the entrance still stands in Sanlao Lane.

三老胡同内留存的一座大门外影壁。

Screens like this one at the entrance of a house were built to block the view of passers-by, or decorate a courtyard. Visitors just entering the courtyard could also make use of the privacy the screen provided to straighten out their outfit or make mental preparation for the meeting with the hosts.

门内的影壁。位于门的入口处,用来遮挡过往行人的视线,并可美化门庭;来访的客人入门后也可借助它的遮掩整理服饰,调整情绪。

A view of a screen from within the courtyard

从院内望屏立于门内的影壁。

An entrance with over-
hanging decorations.
Under the tall roof are
two overhanging "pil-
lars" with wood carv-
ings in between.

西城公用胡同某宅的
垂花门。门上有卷棚式
屋顶,两侧有一对倒悬
的垂柱,两柱之间有雕
花木罩。

Corridors joining an
entrance with over-
hanging decorations

从内院望垂花门及与
其相连的抄手游廊

This house with two courtyards on Shijia Lane was first built in the Qing Dynasty. Today, it still maintains the original layout.

史家胡同某宅内院。此宅始建于清代，为两进院落，现基本仍保持原来的格局。

This archway at 15 East Mianhua Lane combines architectural styles both Chinese and Western. The meticulous brick carvings feature flowers, animals and good luck patterns. Originally the residence of a Qing Dynasty general named Liu, it now houses several families.

东棉花胡同 15 号宅的内宅门。为中西合璧式的拱形券门，门上砖雕精细，雕有花卉、走兽、吉祥图案。该宅原为清末一刘姓将军的住宅，现为多户居民合居。

Work of fine craftsmanship

券门及侧壁上的雕刻

44

The main and master rooms in a quadrangle house. They are larger than other rooms in the house and stand on alleviated foundations. Always facing south, they usually consist of three to four bays and are reserved for the elder members of the family.

四合院的正房。是内宅的主房，一般有三至五间，台基和房屋都比较高大，坐北朝南，供长辈居住。

The house at 19 Fengfu Lane in the East District was the residence of the late author Lao She (1899-1966). A native of Beijing, he lived for sixteen years in this house, where he produced twenty-three novels and dramas, mostly based on the history of Beijing with languages typically spoken by Beijingers.

老舍故居——东城丰富胡同19号宅。现代小说家、戏剧家老舍(公元1899—1966年)生前在这座小院内居住了16年，写出《方珍珠》、《龙须沟》、《西望长安》、《茶馆》等23部作品。

The main rooms of Lao She's residence. He and his wife, Hu Jieqing, planted the two persimmon trees, which gave the courtyard the name of "Red Persimmons Courtyard".

故居的正房。房前有两棵柿树，为老舍与夫人胡絜青手植。小院因树得名，称"丹柿小院"。

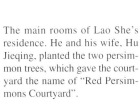

Mei Lanfang, master Peking Opera actor, used to
live here at 9 Huguosi Lane, now Mei Lanfang
Memorial Museum.

护国寺胡同9号宅内分隔内外院的垂花门。该宅为
京剧艺术大师梅兰芳先生故居,今辟为梅兰芳纪念
馆。

Corridor in a house in West Rongxian Lane
西绒线胡同某宅跨院中的游廊

This gate with overhanging decorations in Prince Gong's Palace leads to a garden in the northern part of the premise. Covering 28,000 square meters, the garden has more than twenty scenic attractions.

恭王府花园内的垂花门。花园位于府邸以北，面积2.8万平方米，有20余处景点。

An alley in the palace which consisted of the central, east and west sections, separated by the east and west alleyways. Each section has several courtyards.

府邸中的夹道。府邸由中、东、西三组建筑群组成，每一组皆拥有多进四合院。东西两夹道位于三组建筑群之间。

Corridor in the garden
花园中的游廊

Only part of the wooden windows in quadrangle houses use glass. The rest part is pasted with a particular kind of thick white paper in spring, fall and winter and window screening in summer.

四合院居室的窗大都是木格窗棂，局部镶嵌玻璃，其余部分春、秋、冬三季糊白麻纸，夏季换装透气的窗纱。

Tile ends in quadrangle houses often feature meticulous patterns. Most of the quadrangle houses were built with the same kind of bricks, tiles and timber that had been in use for more than two thousand years. Tile ends with patterns like these were already extensively used during the Qin Dynasty (221-206 BC).

四合院檐头的瓦当。京城四合院的建筑材料是两千多年以来沿用的砖瓦和木材，这种模印花纹的瓦当在两千多年前的秦、汉时期就已广泛运用。

There is a public running water tab in each courtyard. Sometimes, water freezes inside the pipe in winter. The lady is pouring hot water to defrost the pipe water.

每一院内设有公用的自来水龙头，冬季管内的水常常冻结，取用前须浇热水融化。

Traditional interior arrangement. The horizontal chest is for keeping clothes. Porcelain ware and vases in pairs, along with a mirror and clock, serve as interior decorations. Today such arrangement can only be found in very few houses of long-time Beijingers.

传统的室内陈设。木质的横柜，内放衣物；柜上对称地陈列着瓷罐、花瓶、钟、镜等。现在除了极少世居京城的老人，已无人这样布置居室了。

No matter how difficult the living conditions are, residents in Beijing always manage to build up a green environment.

京城人不论居住条件优劣，都能因地制宜营造出一片绿色的空间。

Gourd grown under a house eave
屋檐下的葫芦架

A view outside the rear window
后窗外的风景

To watch snow turning the courtyard into a work of contrasting bright and dark colors from the well-heated room is a great fun for residents in Beijing.

坐在暖融融的屋内，隔窗望着晶莹、绵密的雪花将庭院中的景物勾勒成明暗鲜明的画幅，是京城人冬日里的一桩乐事。

Life of a future football star may well begin from a lane.

未来的"国脚"也许就来自这里。

"Acting as the Bride." Despite all other games of modern times, girls in this lane still favor this traditional game of pleasure seeking.

扮"新娘"。尽管现代化的玩具和游戏方式层出不穷，胡同里的女童却对古老的游戏情有独钟。

Retirees often find pleasure from bird raising. Every morning they take their birds to parks or woods so that the birds can have a moment of pleasure of being in the natural environment.

赋闲的老人多以养鸟自娱，每日清晨要到公园或林木繁茂的地方遛鸟，让笼中的鸟儿享受返归自然的短暂快乐。

This old man, more than seventy years old, from Chuantangmen Lane has been raising birds for several decades.

家住穿堂门胡同的这位七十余岁的老人，几十年与鸟相随相伴，结下了不解之缘。

Nothing can make him happier than strolling with his birds.

乐在其中

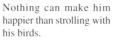

Newspaper stories suggest Beijing residents have a history of several hundred years in raising katydids. Every turn from summer to fall, farmers from the suburbs or neighboring provinces come in Beijing loaded with this kind of longhorned grasshoppers to sell to city kids. The result, katydids singing is heard from every courtyard.

夏秋之交，京郊以及外省农民挑着整担的蝈蝈沿胡同叫卖，引得孩子们争相购买，一时间，家家户户都传出秋虫的鸣叫声。据记载京城人养蝈蝈已有几百年的历史了。

To fly kites in the spring or fall is a favorite sport for many Beijing residents. Colorful kites can be seen in the sky over small lanes.

在春风和畅和秋高气爽的日子里放风筝，是京城人的一件乐事。每逢此时，胡同的上空飘荡着各色各样的风筝。

Three generations living in harmony

三代同堂，其乐融融。

One wedding and the entire lane is filled with a festival mood.

胡同里的婚礼。一家有喜事，左邻右里都来帮忙、祝贺，整条胡同都洋溢着喜庆气氛。

With the introduction of Western way of life, white wedding gowns have replaced traditional wedding apparel, and bridesmaids have been replaced by the best men. Weddings in small lanes are becoming a combination of Chinese and Western practices.

西风东渐，白色的婚纱取代了传统的嫁衣，伴娘改为傧相，胡同里的婚礼已演化成中西合璧式的了！

◁ Merry making in the nuptial room is a traditional practice and still maintains its popularity today.

新婚之夜闹新房是中国传统的婚俗，至今仍是婚礼中不可少的节目，也是婚礼的高潮。

Grandma and her granndchildren
老来孙作伴

To watch street activities, chat about today and
talk about yesterday: a way of life for elderly men
from small lanes.

看街景、谈天说地、感今抚昔，是胡同里老年男
子的消闲方式。

Residents in small lanes near Shishahai Lake are uniquely located. In winter, they go skating or winter swimming and in summer they enjoy swimming and viewing lotus plants.

住在什刹海附近胡同里的居民得天独厚，冬季可在湖上溜冰、在湖中游泳，夏季则可临湖观荷。

Sugarcoated haws are popular on the ice too.
卖冰糖葫芦的小贩直趋冰上，招徕买主。

According to tradition, on every 22nd of the last month on the lunar calendar, people in Beijing paste up Spring Festival couplets and portraits of the door gods. Both the couplets and portraits can be easily found at business stands in lanes, big or small, near Qianmen.

京城旧俗，每年农历十二月二十二日，家家户户须换贴新春联、门神，以迎新纳福。在此前后大街小巷都有售卖春联、门神的摊点。

Helping Daddy to get a filled-up gas cylinder. Some residents use gas as fuel and have to take the empty cylinder for a full one at the gas station in the neighborhood.

帮爸爸换煤气。部分居民用罐装的液化煤气作燃料，罐内煤气用完后，可到距家最近的煤气供应站购买。

A coal mill in a small lane. Coal shaped in this fashion is referred to as the honeycomb coal, which is easy to burn and keep. In the past decade, it has been a major fuel for residents in Beijing.

胡同里的煤厂加工制作蜂窝煤，供应居民。

Advertising for service. The tools used and the way people who sharpen kitchen choppers and scissors advertise are exactly the same as described in folk paintings over a hundred years ago.

敲着响器走街串巷的磨刀剪匠人。其所用的工具与招揽主顾的方式与一百多午前民俗图中所绘毫无二致。

A key cutting stand
修锁配钥匙的小摊，早设晚收。

62

Looking better than they taste
手工制作的糖花味道平平，造型却十分夸张。

Fascinated by a craftsman blowing a syrup figure.
看吹糖人的艺人现场制作，令这个小女孩着了迷。

Making sweet glutinous rice flour dumplings in a lane for the Lantern Festival. The round shape of this delicacy eaten on the 15th day of the 1st month on the lunar calendar symbolizes reunion of the family and smooth sailing in people's life and career. To prepare them, the fillings are made into small balls and shaken in wet glutinous rice flour until the fillings are securely wrapped up. Then they are ready to be boiled and served.

胡同里现摇现卖的元宵摊。中国农历正月十五日是民间的元宵节，这一日晚上家家都要吃元宵，以求一年之中家人团聚，事事圆满。北京制作元宵的方法颇为独特，先将调好的馅搓成团，而后放在浸湿的糯米粉里摇滚，让糯米粉逐层裹于馅外。

A special kind of porridge called literally "flour tea" instantly made and served. To make this traditional Beijing delicacy, wheat flour is first baked and then added with ground peanut, walnut, sesame and sugar. To serve, pour in boiling water and make the flour mix into a thick broth. The copper pot containing boiling water is heated with coal from the center tube. Its mouth is cast into the shape of a dragon head, giving it the name "dragon-head copper pot".

即食即冲的面茶，香气扑鼻。面茶，又名茶汤，是京城传统的风味食品。制法是先将面粉炒熟，搀入捣碎炒熟的花生、核桃仁、芝麻和白糖，吃时将炒面放入碗内，冲入沸水调合成糊状。烧水用特制的大铜壶，壶中有膛，用来燃煤烧水；壶嘴铸成龙头形，俗称"龙嘴大铜壶"。

Fruits from both the north and south of the country are available in stands at entrances of small lanes.

胡同口的水果摊上南北鲜果，四季不断。

Humorous and interesting donkey performance is very popular at temple fairs during the Spring Festival in Beijing.

诙谐、风趣、富有乡土气息的跑驴表演是京城春节庙会上必有的节目。

These performers walking on stilts, doing donkey dance and lion dance are farmers from suburban Beijing. On festival occasions, they often come in the city, bringing their skill and laugh.

踩高跷。踩高跷、跑驴、舞狮的表演者大都是京郊农民业余演出队的成员，他们农闲时排练，遇有节庆前来助兴。

Whole families making dumplings together on the New Year's Eve and eating them at mid-night is an agelong tradition.

京城古俗，除夕之夜家人围坐一处包饺子，待到夜半时煮食，称为"交子"。这一习俗一直沿袭至今。

Sun Baocai (*left*), known as one of the "new magic actors" of Tianqiao area in a comic performance. Lanes near the original Tianqiao Market were where artists of all arts used to perform. Many extremely talented people started their career here. Together they were referred to as "magic performers of Tianqiao".

天桥的新"八大怪"之一孙宝才(左)在表演双簧。天桥一带的胡同是原天桥市场所在地,这里曾是诸般艺人荟萃之处,各个时期都出现过一些身怀绝技、行貌奇特的艺人,人们统称为"天桥八大怪"。

For this man of superb breathing exercise skills, his head remains unhurt after the bricks hitting his head are smashed into pieces.

气功表演劈砖。头顶的砖被劈得四分五裂,顶砖的人却毫发无损。

These old quadrangle houses have to go, too.
正在拆除的四合院群。

Disappearing quadrangle houses
一座即将消失的四合院。

Remaining traces of warm and peaceful family life

残壁上还留有家的温馨。

New houses at Juer Lane have maintained some of the architectural features of traditional quadrangle houses.

菊儿胡同内新建的住宅楼采用了四合院的建筑格局。

Hard to leave!
故宅难舍

图书在版编目（CIP）数据

北京胡同／沈延太，王长青摄．－北京：外文出版社，2002.9
ISBN 7-119-03143-0

Ⅰ.北… Ⅱ.①沈…②王… Ⅲ.城市道路－北京市－画册 Ⅳ.K921-64

中国版本图书馆 CIP 数据核字(2002)第 066835 号

Photos by: Shen Yantai   Wang Changqing
Text by: Liang Bingkun   Liao Pin
Translated by: Huang Youyi
Designed by: Yuan Qing
Edited by: Lan Peijin

摄影：沈延太　王长青
撰文：梁秉堃　廖　频
翻译：黄友义
设计：元　青
责任编辑：兰佩瑾

北京胡同

First Edition 2002

Alleys in Beijing

ISBN 7-119-03143-0

Ⓒ Foreign Languages Press
Published by Foreign Languages Press
24 Baiwanzhuang Road, Beijing 100037, China
Home Page: http://www.flp.com.cn
E-mail Addresses: info@flp.com.cn
　　　　　　　　sales@flp.com.cn
Printed in the People's Republic of China

Ⓒ　外文出版社
外文出版社出版
（中国北京百万庄大街24号）
邮政编码：100037
外文出版社网页：http://www.flp.com.cn
外文出版社电子邮件地址：info@flp.com.cn
　　　　　　　　　　　　sales@flp.com.cn
北京恒智彩印有限公司印刷
外文社照排中心制作
2002 年(24 开)第一版
2002 年第一版第一次印刷
（英汉）
ISBN 7-119-03143-0/J·1618（外）
004800（精）